Wyoming

BY ANN HEINRICHS

Content Adviser: Ellen Stump, Curator of Interpretation, Wyoming State Museum, Cheyenne, Wyoming

Reading Adviser: Dr. Linda D. Labbo, Department of Reading Education, College of Education, The University of Georgia

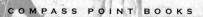 COMPASS POINT BOOKS MINNEAPOLIS, MINNESOTA

Compass Point Books
3109 West 50th Street, #115
Minneapolis, MN 55410

Visit Compass Point Books on the Internet at *www.compasspointbooks.com*
or e-mail your request to *custserv@compasspointbooks.com*

On the cover: Horses and cattle grazing beneath the Teton Range in Grand Teton National Park

Photographs ©: Sharon Gerig/Tom Stack and Associates, cover, 1; Corbis, 3, 29; John Elk III, 5, 12, 30, 31, 38, 39, 40, 48 (top); PhotoDisc, 7, 42, 44 (bottom); Jeff Foott/Tom Stack and Associates, 8; Jim Wark, 9, 15, 23; Digital Vision, 10, 45; Robert McCaw, 13, 43 (top), 44 (top and middle), 47; Spencer Swanger/Tom Stack and Associates, 14; Courtesy Scotts Bluff National Monument, 16, 41; Hulton/Archive by Getty Images, 17, 18, 20, 37; Wyoming State Archives, Department of State Parks and Cultural Resources, 19, 21, 22; Unicorn Stock Photos/Andre Jenny, 25; N. Carter/North Wind Picture Archives, 27; Richard Hamilton Smith, 28; Unicorn Stock Photos/Phyllis Kedl, 32; Corbis/Kevin R. Morris, 33; Courtesy of John MacLachlan, 34 (top), 46; Corbis/Oscar White, 34 (bottom); Photo Network/Howard Folsom, 35; Robesus, Inc., 43 (state flag); One Mile Up, Inc., 43 (state seal).

Editors: E. Russell Primm, Emily J. Dolbear, and Christianne C. Jones
Photo Researcher: Marcie C. Spence
Photo Selector: Linda S. Koutris
Designer: The Design Lab
Cartographer: XNR Productions, Inc.

Library of Congress Cataloging-in-Publication Data
Heinrichs, Ann.
  Wyoming / by Ann Heinrichs.
     p. cm. — (This land is your land)
 Summary: Introduces the geography, history, government, people, culture, and attractions of Wyoming. Includes bibliographical references and index.
   ISBN 0-7565-0359-0 (hardcover : alk. paper)
   1. Wyoming—Juvenile literature. [1. Wyoming.] I. Title. II. Series.
   F761.3.H455 2003
   978.7—dc21   2003005413

Table of Contents

4   Welcome to Wyoming!

6   Mountains, Rivers, and Plains

15 A Trip Through Time

24 Government by the People

27 Wyomingites at Work

31 Getting to Know Wyomingites

35 Let's Explore Wyoming!

41 Important Dates

42 Glossary

42 Did You Know?

43 At a Glance

44 State Symbols

44 Making Wyoming Chili

45 State Song

46 Famous Wyomingites

47 Want to Know More?

48 Index

NOTE: In this book, words that are defined in the glossary are in **bold** the first time they appear in the text.

Wyoming is one of the most scenic places in America. Its snowcapped Rocky Mountains sparkle over the valleys below. Native Americans called these peaks "the backbone of the world."

Wyoming is also home to Yellowstone National Park. Today, millions of visitors enjoy the park's spectacular water jets and mineral pools. Native Americans respected these sites. They were places for healing and holding religious ceremonies.

Wyoming's official nickname is the Equality State. Women in Wyoming could vote long before the whole country granted this right. Wyoming is sometimes called the Cowboy State. Cowboys still ride the range today. Huge cattle ranches spread across the **prairies** where buffalo once roamed.

Wyoming is the nation's top coal producer. Oil, natural gas, and other minerals are plentiful there, too. Now let's explore this land of ancient history and natural beauty!

▲ Bison, or buffalo, graze at Jackson Hole, which is at the foot of the Teton Range.

Wyoming is one of the Rocky Mountain states in the western United States. All its borders are straight lines. To the north is Montana. Idaho lies to the west, and Utah borders Wyoming's southwest corner. Colorado lies to the south. South Dakota and Nebraska border eastern Wyoming.

Two great American land regions meet in Wyoming— the Great Plains and the Rocky Mountains. Eastern Wyoming lies within the Great Plains. The Rocky Mountains, or Rockies, cover western Wyoming.

The grassy prairies of the Great Plains stretch as far as the eye can see. Thousands of cattle and sheep graze there. The Black Hills cover Wyoming's northeastern corner. Devils Tower is one of the region's strange rock formations.

The Rocky Mountains run from north to south. Wyoming's Rockies include the Laramie, Absaroka, Wind River, and Teton ranges. The snowcapped Teton Range rises high

▲ Devils Tower is located in the Black Hills of northeast Wyoming.

▲ Grand Teton National Park has beautiful mountains, lakes, and wildflowers.

over Jackson Hole. Many basins, or flat areas, lie between the mountain ranges. Cattle and sheep graze in several of these basins.

Winding through Wyoming's Rockies is the Continental Divide, which is a dividing point for North America's waters. West of the Divide, waters flow toward the Pacific Ocean. East of the Divide, they flow toward the Mississippi River.

One region in Wyoming is neither east nor west of the Continental Divide. This region in south-central Wyoming is the Great Divide Basin. It is also called the Red

Desert. When rain falls there, it doesn't flow in any direction. It just soaks right into the ground.

Yellowstone National Park is in Wyoming's northwest corner. Just below Earth's surface is an area of **magma** called Yellowstone's "hot spot." The hot spot is responsible for the

▲ **The northwest edge of the Contintental Divide in Fremont County**

many hot springs, steam vents, mudpots, and colorful mineral pools found in Yellowstone. Mudpots are boiling pools of mineral mud. Some are stinky! They give off hydrogen sulfide, or "rotten-egg gas."

The hot spot also powers Yellowstone's geysers. Yellowstone has more geysers than anywhere else in the world. Geysers are springs that spray hot water and steam high into

▲ **Minerva Spring is a hot spring in Yellowstone National Park.**

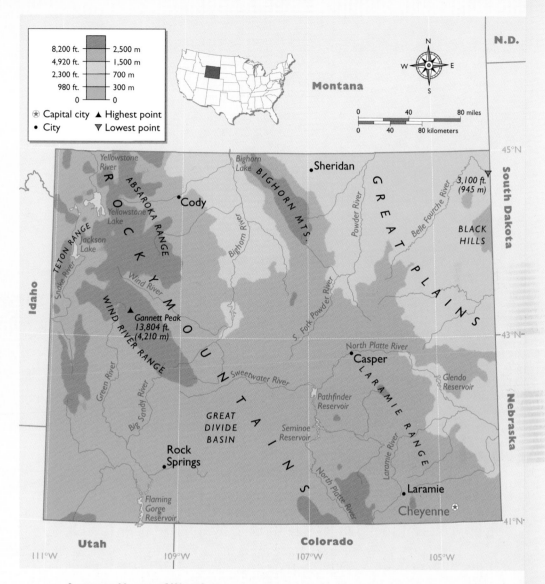

Montana

N.D.

South Dakota

Nebraska

Colorado

Utah

Idaho

Yellowstone River

R O C K Y   M O U N T A I N S

ABSAROKA RANGE

TETON RANGE

Yellowstone Lake

Jackson Lake

Snake River

Wind River

Cody

Bighorn Lake

BIGHORN MTS.

Sheridan

Bighorn River

Powder River

G R E A T   P L A I N S

Belle Fourche River

3,100 ft. (945 m) ▼

BLACK HILLS

▲ Gannett Peak 13,804 ft. (4,210 m)

WIND RIVER RANGE

Green River

Big Sandy River

Sweetwater River

S. Fork Powder River

North Platte River

Casper

LARAMIE RANGE

Glendo Reservoir

Pathfinder Reservoir

GREAT DIVIDE BASIN

Seminoe Reservoir

Rock Springs

North Platte River

Laramie River

Laramie

Cheyenne ⊛

Flaming Gorge Reservoir

45°N
43°N
41°N

111°W   109°W   107°W   105°W

0   40   80 miles
0   40   80 kilometers

▲ **A topographic map of Wyoming**

the air. Yellowstone's most famous geyser is named Old
Faithful. It is called Old Faithful because its eruptions are
so regular and predictable.

▲ Bighorn Canyon

Over time, some rivers have carved out canyons with steep, colorful rock walls. Beautiful canyons rise over the Laramie, Snake, Yellowstone, and Wind Rivers. Dams on these rivers formed lakes in some of the canyons. Montana's dam on the Bighorn River created Bighorn Canyon. The Green River flows through Flaming **Gorge** into Utah. The Flaming Gorge Dam backs up the river water to create a large artificial lake.

Mountain lions, bison, and moose live in the Yellowstone area. Endangered animals such as grizzly bears and gray wolves also live there. Bighorn sheep make their homes in the northern mountains.

Many animals roam through Wyoming's basin regions. They include antelope, coyotes, jackrabbits, and wildcats. No other state has as many pronghorn antelope. Wyoming also has the world's largest single herd of elk. Rare trumpeter and whistler swans live in Wyoming, too.

Wyoming has warm summers and cold winters.

▲ Bighorn sheep live in the northern Rocky Mountains.

▲ Trumpeter swans are a rare breed of swan that live in Wyoming.

However, the mountains are always cooler than the lowlands. Even in the summer, the higher mountain regions are chilly. Temperatures can drop below freezing, and it can snow in July! Yellowstone and the northwestern mountains have the coldest weather and receive the most snow. Wyoming's basins are arid, or dry. They get little rainfall. Wyoming's Great Divide Basin is known for its high winds.

▲ **A bison wanders through snow-covered Yellowstone National Park.**

Prehistoric people lived in Wyoming thousands of years ago. One group laid out a stone shrine called the Medicine Wheel. This sacred site is located alongside Medicine Mountain near Lovell. Near Lusk, many groups mined quartzite, jasper, and agate. They made tools from these minerals and traded them hundreds of miles away.

Later, many groups of Plains Indians lived in Wyoming. Among these groups were the Arapaho, Cheyenne, Crow, Shoshone, Sioux, and Ute. They lived by hunting wild game and by gathering wild fruits and plants. They moved from place to place, following the herds.

The Wyoming region became part of the United States in 1803 with the

▲ **The Medicine Wheel**

▲ Settlers in covered wagons heading toward Wind River Valley in present-day Lander during the 1800s

Louisiana Purchase. Then American fur trappers and traders began exploring the area. John Colter explored the Yellowstone region in 1807. Colter was probably the first white American in present-day Wyoming. Robert Stuart led a group of traders across the Rocky Mountains in 1812. He found that South Pass was a good way through the mountains.

Many more explorers set up trading posts in the region. In 1834, William Sublette and Robert Campbell opened Fort William on the plains of eastern Wyoming. It was later named Fort Laramie. This was Wyoming's first permanent trading post.

Many westbound travelers passed through Wyoming in the mid-1800s. They followed the Oregon Trail, the California Trail, or the Mormon Trail. All these routes crossed the Rockies through South Pass.

▲ Traders, soldiers, and Native Americans head toward Fort Laramie in 1845.

The Union Pacific Railroad reached Wyoming in the late 1860s. New towns sprang up along the railroad tracks. They included Cheyenne, Laramie, Rock Springs, Green River, and Evanston.

Cattle ranching became an important business. Texas cowboys drove their herds of cattle into Wyoming. The cattle had room to graze over acres of wide-open range.

▲ **The Union Pacific Railroad in Wyoming in 1867**

▲ **Esther Hobart Morris**

Wyoming was once part of the huge Dakota Territory. Wyoming Territory was created in 1868. In 1869, the territory granted women the right to vote and to hold public offices. Women did not have these rights anywhere else in the country. In 1870, Esther Hobart Morris became **justice of the peace** in South Pass. She was America's first female judge. Louisa Swain of Laramie became the first woman to vote in 1870.

However, things did not go as well for Wyoming's Native Americans. Settlers kept moving onto or traveling through Native Americans' lands. Their journeys over these lands drove animals away from the Native Americans' hunting grounds. Conflicts broke out, and the U.S. Army often became involved. By the 1870s, Wyoming's Native Americans were either driven out or confined to **reservations.**

In 1872, Congress made Yellowstone the country's first national park. As visitors poured in to see it, Wyoming's tourism industry began. Wyoming became the forty-fourth U.S. state in 1890.

Ranching became such a big business that it led to the Johnson County War. Powerful, wealthy ranchers were called cattle barons. They began to accuse small-scale ranchers of stealing their cattle. In 1892, the cattle barons

▲ **A rainbow over Yellowstone Lake in Yellowstone National Park**

▲ Gunmen hired by cattle barons to kill small-scale ranchers in 1892 were held prisoner at Fort D. A. Russell.

hired gunmen to kill these ranchers. Two were killed before lawmen stopped them. Later, cattle ranchers fought with sheep ranchers over grazing lands.

Wyomingites built many dams on their rivers in the early 1900s. This brought **irrigation** water to much of the state's dry land. Dams also provided drinking water for

▲ Nellie Tayloe Ross was America's
first female governor.

many communities. Some Wyomingites use the reservoirs formed by dams for fishing and boating. Wyoming's first oil well was drilled in the 1880s. The oil industry became a booming business in 1912, when oil was discovered outside of Casper.

Women in Wyoming continued to enjoy their rights. In 1925, Nellie Tayloe Ross became Wyoming's governor. She was America's first elected female governor.

Wyoming products were useful during World War II (1939–1945). The state provided beef, oil, and coal as part of the war effort. After the war, Wyoming began mining uranium and **trona.** They added to the state's booming mineral industry. An oil shortage in the 1970s and concern for the environment boosted Wyoming's coal industry. Wyoming's coal burns cleaner than other coal.

Today, Wyoming's mineral industry is still strong. However, state leaders know it's not a good idea to depend on one industry. They are working to expand other businesses in the state. Meanwhile, taxes on mineral production provide a great benefit. This money is used to improve public services for Wyoming's people.

▲ **An open-pit coal mine in Sweetwater County**

Government by the People

Today, no one is surprised to see women voting. In the 1800s, however, women could not take part in their government— unless they lived in Wyoming. In 1869, Wyoming Territory passed some new laws. They granted women the right to vote, hold public office, own property, and serve on juries. That's why Wyoming's nickname is the Equality State. More than fifty years passed before all American women could vote. In 1920, the Nineteenth **Amendment** to the U.S. **Constitution** granted voting rights to all women.

Women continue to serve in Wyoming's state government. The state government is divided into three branches— legislative, executive, and judicial. The U.S. government is organized the same way. Having three branches of government creates a good balance of power.

The legislative branch consists of Wyoming's legislature. Its job is to make the state's laws. Voters in each district elect their lawmakers. The state legislature has two houses, or sections—a thirty-member senate and a sixty-member house of representatives. They all meet in the state capitol in Cheyenne.

Wyoming's governor heads the executive branch. This branch makes sure the state's laws are carried out. Voters elect a governor every four years. The governor can serve only two terms within a sixteen-year period. Many other officers take care of executive duties. The voters elect some of these officers, and the governor appoints others.

The judicial branch decides whether laws have been broken and how criminals should be punished. Wyoming's judges

▲ **The state capitol in Cheyenne**

make up the judicial branch. The judges hear cases in court. The state supreme court is Wyoming's highest court. It consists of five justices, or judges.

When Wyoming became a territory, it had only five counties. Today, it has twenty-three. Voters elect three to five county commissioners. Most cities elect a mayor and a city council. Casper and Laramie, however, have city managers. A commu-

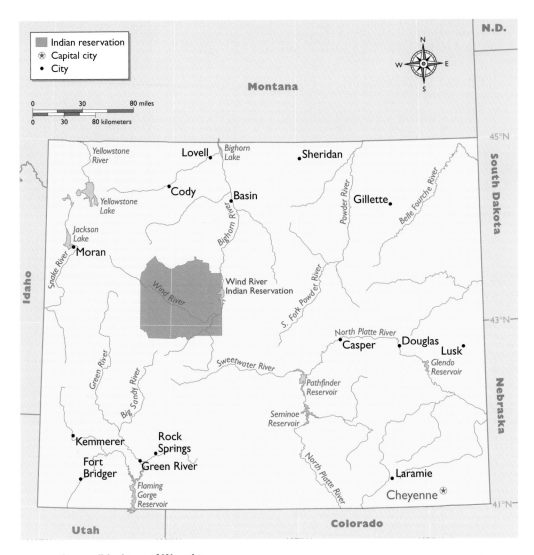

Indian reservation
Capital city
City

0   30   80 miles
0   30   80 kilometers

N.D.

Montana

45°N

Yellowstone River

Lovell

Bighorn Lake

Sheridan

South Dakota

Cody

Basin

Gillette

Belle Fourche River

Powder River

Yellowstone Lake

Jackson Lake

Moran

Snake River

Bighorn River

Wind River

Wind River Indian Reservation

S. Fork Powder River

43°N

Idaho

Green River

North Platte River

Casper

Douglas

Lusk

Glendo Reservoir

Sweetwater River

Big Sandy River

Pathfinder Reservoir

Nebraska

Seminoe Reservoir

Kemmerer

Rock Springs

Green River

Fort Bridger

Flaming Gorge Reservoir

North Platte River

Laramie

Cheyenne

41°N

Utah

Colorado

▲ **A geopolitical map of Wyoming**

nity with fewer than four thousand people is called a town.

In most states, citizens pay a state income tax. However,
Wyomingites don't because the state collects so much from
mineral taxes.

Mining is more valuable to Wyoming than it is to other states. Mining generates more than one-fourth of the gross state product (GSP). The GSP is the total value of everything Wyoming produces. No other state mines more coal than Wyoming. Wyoming is also a leader in petroleum (oil) and natural gas.

Wyoming is the number-one state for trona and bentonite, too. The world's largest known deposits of trona are in Wyoming. Trona is a mineral that is used to make glass, paper,

▲ **An oil well in Thunder Basin in northeast Wyoming**

▲ Beef cattle bring in most of Wyoming's farm income.

soap, baking soda, and artificial fibers. Bentonite is a type of clay that can absorb liquids. It is used to drill for oil and to make chemicals and kitty litter.

Wyoming's ranches and farms are the biggest in the country. Cattle and sheep graze on about half of all Wyoming's land. Beef cattle bring in most of the state's farm income. Wyoming is also known for its sheep and wool. Only Texas produces more wool than Wyoming. Hogs and dairy cattle are valuable farm animals, too.

Most crops are grown with the help of irrigation. Sugarbeets are the leading crop. Hay is another important farm product.

It's mostly used to feed cattle and other animals. Other valuable crops include barley, corn, pinto beans, and potatoes.

Many of Wyoming's factories process the state's natural products. The leading factory activity is making soda ash from trona. Refining, or cleaning, petroleum is another important activity. Other factories make food products, metal goods,

▲ **Hay is one of Wyoming's most important crops.**

This park ranger at Devils Tower National Monument is a service worker.

cement, and wood products.

Most Wyomingites have service jobs. Instead of selling goods, they sell their services. Some service workers have jobs in the tourist industry. Some work in hotels, restaurants, or ski resorts. Others work on dude ranches. They are tourist sites where visitors can find out what life on a ranch is like by participating in chores and other activities. Gas stations, stores, banks, hospitals, and schools all employ service workers. Wyoming could not run smoothly without service workers.

Getting to Know Wyomingites

Which state has the smallest population? If you guessed Wyoming, you're right! Fewer than half a million people lived there in 2000. Wyomingites have a lot of "elbow room," too. Only Alaska, the largest state, has fewer people per square mile.

About two out of three residents live in cities or towns. Even the cities are small, though. Only Cheyenne, the largest city, has more than fifty thousand people. The next-largest cities are Casper, Laramie, and Gillette.

▲ **A ranch in northern Wyoming**

▲ A Native American woman from the Wind River Indian Reservation performs a traditional dance.

People from several nations came to Wyoming in the 1800s. They included Germans, Swedes, Greeks, Italians, Poles, and people from many other countries. People from the Basque regions of Spain and France came to herd sheep. Chinese people helped build railroads. Rock Springs was known for its mix of people from different nations. Most of these people came to work in the nearby coal mines.

Today, eleven out of twelve Wyomingites are **descendants** of Europeans. Asian, African-American, and **Hispanic** people live in Wyoming, too. The state's largest Native American groups are the Shoshone and the Arapaho. Most live on the Wind River Indian Reservation.

Cowboy life and cowboy culture are found throughout Wyoming. There are often rodeos, especially in the summer. Cheyenne Frontier Days is the world's biggest outdoor rodeo. Others include the Cody Nite Rodeo and the Sheridan

▲ Actors in traditional Native American dress reenact Wyoming's frontier days at the Green River Rendezvous in Pinedale.

WYO Rodeo. The Wyoming State Fair and Rodeo takes place in Douglas.

People celebrate fur-trapping days at the Fort Bridger Rendezvous (RON-day-voo). Fur trappers used to meet once a year for a rendezvous. It was a big reunion for trading, swapping stories, and renewing friendships. Wyomingites also hold the Green River Rendezvous, the Bear River Mountain Man Rendezvous, and many others.

Skiers from all over the world enjoy Wyoming's ski areas. Jackson Hole, Snow King Mountain, and Meadowlark are popular ski resorts. Dude ranches are a big attraction, too. Millions of people visit Wyoming's national parks. They hike through the wilderness and admire the mountains and wildlife.

Two popular children's book authors came from Wyoming—Mary O'Hara and Patricia MacLachlan. O'Hara wrote about children's lives on Wyoming's wide-open ranges. *My Friend Flicka* (1941) is her most popular story. MacLachlan won the Newbery Medal for her book *Sarah, Plain and Tall* (1985).

James Cash Penney opened a little store called the Golden Rule Store in Kemmerer in 1902. He had two rules. The first was "cash only." The second was the Golden Rule—"Do unto others as you would have them do unto you." Penney kept opening more stores. They became the JCPenney department stores.

Everyone considered Russian wrestler Alexander Karelin unbeatable in the 2000 Olympics in Sydney, Australia. It took Rulon Gardner, the son of a dairy farmer from Afton, to beat him. Defeating Karelin won Gardner the gold medal in the heavy-weight division of Greco-Roman wrestling.

▲ J. C. Penney

Let's Explore Wyoming!

If you love the outdoors, you'll love Wyoming. It's one of America's most popular vacation spots. The top "must-see" site is Yellowstone National Park. Moose and protected herds of bison, or buffalo, wander through the park. You can watch geysers hurl boiling water into the air. You'll hear hissing steam shoot out of the ground and will smell gases rising from bubbling mudpots. The wild colors of mineral pools are an amazing sight to behold.

Yellowstone is beautiful, but it can also be dangerous. It is always important to be careful while exploring the park, for your own safety and for the good of the animal and plant life there.

Just south of Yellowstone is Grand Teton National Park. Its snowcapped peaks rise high over the Jackson Hole valley. Grizzly bears, mountain lions, bison, and

▲ **Bison near Nez Perce Creek in Yellowstone National Park**

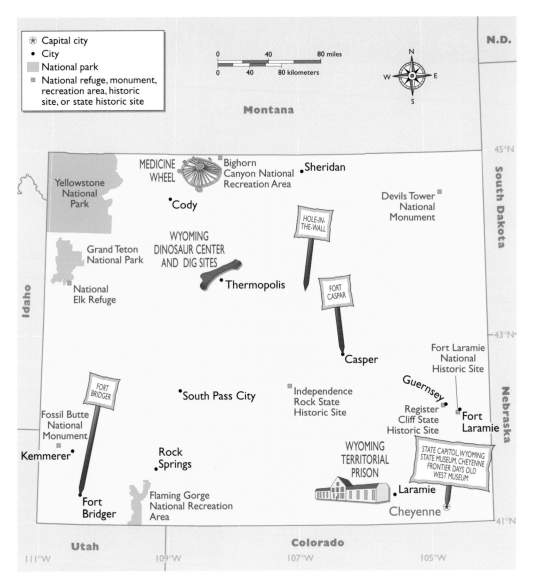

Legend:
- ✴ Capital city
- • City
- ▪ National park
- ▪ National refuge, monument, recreation area, historic site, or state historic site

0 — 40 — 80 miles
0 — 40 — 80 kilometers

N.D.

Montana

45°N

South Dakota

Yellowstone National Park

MEDICINE WHEEL

Bighorn Canyon National Recreation Area

•Sheridan

Devils Tower National Monument

•Cody

Grand Teton National Park

WYOMING DINOSAUR CENTER AND DIG SITES

HOLE-IN-THE-WALL

National Elk Refuge

•Thermopolis

FORT CASPAR

43°N

•Casper

Fort Laramie National Historic Site

FORT BRIDGER

•South Pass City

Independence Rock State Historic Site

Guernsey

Register Cliff State Historic Site

Fort Laramie

Fossil Butte National Monument

Kemmerer•

Rock Springs

WYOMING TERRITORIAL PRISON

STATE CAPITOL, WYOMING STATE MUSEUM, CHEYENNE FRONTIER DAYS OLD WEST MUSEUM

Fort Bridger

Flaming Gorge National Recreation Area

•Laramie

Cheyenne

41°N

Idaho

Nebraska

Utah

Colorado

111°W   109°W   107°W   105°W

▲ **Places to visit in Wyoming**

moose roam in the forests. Thousands of elk spend their win-

ters in Jackson Hole's National Elk Refuge.

Bighorn Canyon and Flaming Gorge are spectacular

recreation areas. Their red-and-orange-striped cliffs rise high over the waters. Both sites are surrounded by nature areas that you can explore.

Butch Cassidy (front row, right), the Sundance Kid (front row, left), and other American outlaws in 1885

The Medicine Wheel is on Medicine Mountain in Bighorn National Forest. It's a great circle of stones. Rows of stones stretch out from the center like the spokes of a wheel. Ancient people built this as a site for religious ceremonies.

Hole-in-the-Wall is located near Kaycee. In the late 1800s, many famous outlaws would hide out there. Maybe you've heard of some of them. They included Butch Cassidy and Harry Longbaugh—also called the Sundance Kid.

Fossil Butte National Monument is near Kemmerer. It was the bottom of an **inland** sea 50 million years ago. Thousands of plant and animal fossils are left in the rocks there.

Devils Tower National Monument in the Black Hills looks like a huge tree stump. To Native Americans, Devils Tower is a

▲ Fort Caspar was once a stop for riders who worked for the Pony Express mail service.

sacred place for prayer. It is made of volcanic rock. There are many theories about how it formed, but no one is certain.

In Cheyenne, you can tour the state capitol and watch the lawmakers in action. Nearby is the Wyoming State Museum. It explores the state's history. The Cheyenne Frontier Days Old West Museum is in Cheyenne, too. The Wyoming Territorial Prison in Laramie is now a museum. You can learn about the famous outlaws who ended up in this prison.

U.S. Army forts protected travelers along the Oregon Trail. Wyoming's major fort was Fort Laramie. Many of its original buildings are still standing. Mountain man Jim Bridger opened

Fort Bridger in 1843. Fort Caspar was also a stop for the Pony Express mail service. All these forts welcome visitors.

Independence Rock and Register Cliff were landmarks along the Oregon Trail. Thousands of pioneers scratched their names into these rocks. Near Guernsey, you can see the ruts, or grooves, left by the pioneers' wagon wheels.

South Pass City developed near the famous pass through the Rocky Mountains. It became a "boom town" when gold was found there. Now you can visit its old saloon, jail, and dance hall.

Do you know what *Thermopolis* means? It comes from the Latin word "hot" and the Greek word for "city." The com-

▲ **Independence Rock on the Oregon Trail**

▲ The skeleton of a triceratops at the Wyoming Dinosaur Center in Thermopolis

bination means "hot city." That's the perfect name for Wyoming's town of Thermopolis. It has the world's largest hot-water springs. People come to bathe in the springs for their health. Thermopolis is also home to the Wyoming Dinosaur Center and Dig Sites. There you'll find life-sized dinosaur skeletons—and you can go digging for bones yourself!

Wyoming has much more than natural beauty. It's a place where millions of years of history come alive.

Important Dates

1742– 1743 François Louis Verendrye enters present-day Wyoming.

1807 John Colter explores the Yellowstone region.

1812 Robert Stuart finds a way across the Rocky Mountains at South Pass.

1833 Captain Benjamin de Bonneville maps the Wyoming area and builds Fort Bonneville.

1834 William Sublette and Robert Campbell open Fort William, which is later named Fort Laramie.

1842 Jim Bridger establishes Fort Bridger, and John C. Fremont explores Wyoming.

1868 Wyoming Territory is created.

1869 Wyoming grants women the right to vote, own property, and be elected to public offices.

1872 Yellowstone National Park becomes America's first national park.

1890 Wyoming becomes the forty-fourth U.S. state on July 10.

1892 The Johnson County War takes place.

1906 Devils Tower becomes the country's first national monument.

1925 Nellie Tayloe Ross becomes America's first elected woman governor.

1951– 1952 Uranium deposits are found in Wyoming.

1960 The country's first intercontinental ballistic missile base opens near Cheyenne.

1988 Forest fires sweep through much of Yellowstone National Park.

1995 Wolves are reintroduced in Yellowstone National Park.

Glossary

amendment—a change added on to a document

Constitution—a written document explaining the basic laws of the United States

descendants—a person's children, grandchildren, great-grandchildren, and their offspring

gorge—a deep valley with steep sides

Hispanic—people of Mexican, South American, and other Spanish-speaking cultures

inland—not on or near the coast, but inside a country

irrigation—bringing water to crops by digging canals or ditches

justice of the peace—a public official with the power to make legal decisions in minor cases and to perform marriages

magma—hot, melted rock

prairies—flat or rolling grasslands

prehistoric—occurring before people began recording history

reservations—large areas of land set aside for Native Americans

trona—a mineral that yields soda ash, or sodium carbonate

Did You Know?

★ Yellowstone National Park became America's first national park in 1872. It is the nation's largest national park.

★ Shoshone National Forest became the country's first national forest in 1891.

★ Devils Tower was declared the first national monument in 1906. Movie fans will recognize it from the 1977 science fiction film *Close Encounters of the Third Kind.*

★ Nellie Tayloe Ross was the first woman governor (1925–1927) in the United States and also the first woman to head the U.S. Mint (1933–1953).

★ The U.S. government owns about half of Wyoming's land. That includes national parks, national forests, and other government lands.

★ The name *Wyoming* comes from the Delaware Indians. It means "upon the great plain."

State capital: Cheyenne

State motto: Equal Rights

State nickname: Equality State

Statehood: July 10, 1890; forty-fourth state

Land area: 97,105 square miles (251,502 square kilometers); **rank:** ninth

Highest point: Gannett Peak, 13,804 feet (4,210 meters) above sea level

Lowest point: Belle Fourche River in Crook County, 3,100 feet (945 m) above sea level

Highest recorded temperature: 115°F (46°C) at Basin on August 8, 1983

Lowest recorded temperature: –66°F (–54°C) at Moran on February 9, 1933

Average January temperature: 19°F (–7°C)

Average July temperature: 67°F (19°C)

Population in 2000: 493,782; **rank:** fiftieth

Largest cities in 2000: Cheyenne (53,011), Casper (49,644), Laramie (27,204), Gillette (19,646)

Factory products: Chemicals, petroleum products, food products

Farm products: Beef cattle, sheep and wool, hay

Mining products: Coal, petroleum, natural gas, trona, bentonite

State flag: Wyoming's state flag has a white figure of a bison in the center. The state seal is branded on the center of the bison figure. The bison is set against a blue background with a thin white border and a wide red border around it. Blue stands for the color of the sky and mountains. White stands for purity and honesty. Red stands for Native Americans and for the blood of pioneers who gave their lives working the soil.

State seal: The state seal shows a female figure with a banner reading Equal Rights. She symbolizes the rights granted to women by the government of Wyoming. Beside her are two men, representing the state's livestock and mining industries. Two pillars bear banners reading Oil, Mines, Livestock, and Grain—major industries in Wyoming. Beneath the woman is an American eagle perched on a shield. At the bottom are two dates—1869, the date Wyoming Territory was organized, and 1890, the date of statehood.

State abbreviations: Wyo. (traditional); WY (postal)

State Symbols

State bird: Western meadowlark

State flower: Indian paintbrush

State tree: Plains cottonwood

State mammal: Bison

State fish: Cutthroat trout

State reptile: Horned toad

State gemstone: Jade

State dinosaur: Triceratops

State fossil: Knightia

State sport: Rodeo

Making Wyoming Chili

Many Wyomingites like hearty foods, such as chili.

The state's cattle and sheep provide the main ingredient.

Makes eight servings.

INGREDIENTS:

3 pounds ground beef, lamb, or mutton

1/4 cup dried onions

1/4 cup chili powder

2 tablespoons Worcestershire sauce

1 teaspoon garlic powder

1 teaspoon oregano

1 can tomatoes

1 can tomato sauce

Salt and pepper to suit your taste

DIRECTIONS:

Make sure an adult helps you with the hot stove.
Break up the meat in a large pot. Over medium heat,
stir until it's brown. Pour off the fat. Add all the other
ingredients. Lower the heat and simmer. Keep checking to
see if it's getting too dry. If it is, add a little water. Chili
should be ready to eat after about two hours.

"Wyoming"

Words by C. E. Winter, music by G. E. Knapp

In the far and mighty West,
Where the crimson sun seeks rest,
There's a growing splendid State that
lies above,
On the breast of this great land;
Where the massive Rockies stand,
There's Wyoming young and strong, the
State I love!

Chorus:
Wyoming, Wyoming! Land of the sunlight
clear!
Wyoming, Wyoming! Land that we hold
so dear!
Wyoming, Wyoming! Precious art thou
and thine!
Wyoming, Wyoming! Beloved State of mine!

In the flowers wild and sweet,
Colors rare and perfumes meet;
There's the columbine so pure, the
daisy too,
Wild the rose and red it springs,
White the button and its rings,
Thou art loyal for they're red and white
and blue.

Where thy peaks with crowned head,
Rising till the sky they wed,
Sit like snow queens ruling wood and
stream and plain;
'Neath thy granite bases deep,
'Neath thy bosom's broadened sweep,
Lie the riches that have gained and brought
thee fame.

Other treasures thou dost hold,
Men and women thou dost mould,
True and earnest are the lives that thou
dost raise,
Strengthen thy children though dost teach,
Nature's truth thou givest to each,
Free and noble are thy workings and
thy ways.

In the nation's banner free
There's one star that has for me
A radiance pure and splendor like the sun;
Mine it is, Wyoming's star,
Home it leads me near or far;
O Wyoming! All my heart and love
you've won!

James Bridger (1804–1881) was a trapper and guide who explored the Rocky Mountain region. He built Fort Bridger in 1842.

Richard Cheney (1941–) became vice president under President George W. Bush in 2001. He was born in Nebraska and grew up in Casper. His wife, Lynne, also grew up in Casper.

"Buffalo Bill" Cody (1846–1917) founded the town of Cody. He was famous for his Wild West Show. Cody was born in Iowa.

John Colter (1775?–1813) was a fur trader and explorer. In 1807, he was the first white American to enter Wyoming.

Rulon Gardner (1971–) won the 2000 Olympic gold medal in Greco-Roman wrestling. He was born in Afton.

Curt Gowdy (1919–) is a sportscaster for professional football and baseball games. In 1970, he became the first sportscaster to receive the George Foster Peabody award for excellence in broadcasting. There is a state park named after him between Cheyenne and Laramie. Gowdy was born in Green River.

Patricia MacLachlan (1938–) is an author of children's books. She won the Newbery Medal for *Sarah, Plain and Tall* (1985). MacLachlan (pictured above left) was born in Cheyenne.

Esther Hobart Morris (1814–1902) was America's first female judge. She became justice of the peace for South Pass in 1870. She also worked for women's voting rights. She was born in New York.

Mary O'Hara (1885–1980) wrote many books about life in Wyoming, including *My Friend Flicka* (1941). She was born in New Jersey and later lived in Wyoming.

J. C. Penney (1875–1971) started the JCPenney department stores in Kemmerer. He was born in Missouri.

Nellie Tayloe Ross (1876–1977) was Wyoming's governor from 1925 to 1927. She was the nation's first woman governor and also the first woman to head the U.S. Mint (1933–1953). She was born in Missouri.

Gerry Spence (1929–) is one of the most famous defense lawyers in the United States. He was born in Laramie.

Francis Warren (1844–1929) became Wyoming's first governor in 1890. He soon became a U.S. senator from Wyoming (1890–1929). Warren was born in Massachusetts.

Chief Washakie (1798–1900) was a Shoshone leader. He worked to get land and social services for his people. His policy of peace toward the U.S. government helped the Shoshone gain a large reservation in central Wyoming.

Want to Know More?

At the Library

Hanson-Harding, Alexandra. *Wyoming.* Danbury, Conn.: Children's Press, 2003.

Joseph, Paul. *Wyoming.* Edina, Minn.: Abdo & Daughters, 1998.

Maynard, Charles W. *Fort Laramie.* New York: PowerKids Press, 2002.

Meister, Cari. *Yellowstone National Park.* Edina, Minn.: Abdo & Daughters, 2001.

O'Hara, Mary. *My Friend Flicka.* New York: HarperFestival, 2003.

Wooldridge, Connie Nordhielm, and Jacqueline Rogers (illustrator). *When Esther Morris Headed West: Women, Wyoming, and the Right to Vote.* New York: Holiday House, 2001.

On the Web

Wyoming Welcomes You
http://www.state.wy.us
To learn about Wyoming's history, government, and economy

Wyoming Tourism
http://www.wyomingtourism.org
To find out about Wyoming's events, activities, and sights

Wyoming State Museum
http://wyomuseum.state.wy.us
To learn about Wyoming's history

Through the Mail

Wyoming Business Council
Travel and Tourism Division
214 West 15th Street
Cheyenne, W Y 82002
For information on travel and interesting sights in Wyoming

Wyoming Division of Economic Analysis
1807 Capitol Avenue, Suite 206
Cheyenne, W Y 82002
For information on Wyoming's economy

On the Road

Wyoming State Capitol
200 West 24th Street
Cheyenne, W Y 82002
307/777-7220
To visit Wyoming's state capitol

Wyoming State Museum
2301 Central Avenue
Cheyenne, W Y 82002
307/777-7022
To see artifacts related to Wyoming's history

Absaroka Range, 6
animal life, 5, 13, 35–36

basin regions, 6, 8, 13
Bighorn Canyon, 12, 36–37
Bighorn National Forest, 37
Black Hills, 6
borders, 6
Bridger, Jim, 38–39
Butte, Fossil, 37

California Trail, 17
Campbell, Robert, 16
Casper, 25, 31
Cassidy, Butch, 37
cattle barons, 20–21
Cheyenne, 18, 25, 31, 38
Cheyenne Frontier Days, 32, 38
climate, 13–14
Colter, John, 16
Continental Divide, 8

Dakota Territory, 19
dams, 12, 21–22
Devils Tower, 6, 37–38
dude ranches, 30, 33

ethnic groups, 32
Evanston, 18
executive branch of govern-
    ment, 24, 25

farming, 28–29
Flaming Gorge, 12, 36–37
Fort Bridger, 39
Fort Caspar, 39
Fort Laramie, 17, 38
Fort William, 17

fur trade, 16, 33
Gardner, Rulon, 34
geysers, 10–11, 35
Gillette, 31
Grand Teton National Park, 35
Great Divide Basin, 8–9, 14
Great Plains, 6
Green River, 12, 18

Hole-in-the-Wall, 37
"hot spot," 9–11
hot-water springs, 10, 40

income tax, 26
Independence Rock, 39
irrigation, 21–22, 28

JCPenney department
    stores, 34
Jackson Hole, 6
Johnson County War, 20–21
judicial branch of govern-
    ment, 24, 25

Karelin, Alexander, 34

Laramie, 18, 25, 31, 38
Laramie Range, 6
legislative branch of govern-
    ment, 24–25
livestock, 5, 6, 8, 18, 28
local government, 25–26.
    See also state govern-
    ment.
Longbaugh, Harry
    "Sundance Kid," 37

MacLachlan, Patricia, 34

manufacturing, 22, 29–30
Medicine Mountain, 15, 37
Medicine Wheel, 15, 37
mining, 4, 15, 22–23,
    27–28
Mormon Trail, 17
Morris, Esther Hobart, 19
mountains, 4, 6, 13, 14, 15,
    16, 17, 33, 37, 39

National Elk Refuge, 36
Native Americans, 4, 15,
    19, 32, 37–38
Nineteenth Amendment, 24

O'Hara, Mary, 34
oil industry, 22
Old Faithful geyser, 11
Old West Museum, 38
Oregon Trail, 17, 38, 39

Penney, James Cash, 34
petroleum industries, 4, 22,
    29
Pony Express, 39
population, 31
prehistoric cultures, 15

ranching, 5, 18, 20–21, 28,
    33
Red Desert. See Great
    Divide Basin.
Register Cliff, 39
reservations, 19, 32
rivers, 6, 12, 21
Rock Springs, 18
Rocky Mountains, 4, 6, 16,
    17
rodeos, 32–33

Ross, Nellie Tayloe, 22

service industries, 30
skiing, 33
South Pass, 17
South Pass City, 39
state capital, 18, 25, 31, 38
state capitol, 25, 38
state government, 24–25.
    See also local govern-
    ment.
statehood, 20
Stuart, Robert, 16
Sublette, William, 16
Swain, Louisa, 19

Teton Range, 6
Thermopolis, 39–40
tourism, 20, 30
trading posts, 16, 17

Union Pacific Railroad, 18

voting rights, 4, 19, 24

Wind River Range, 6
Wind River Reservation, 32
World War II, 22
Wyoming Dinosaur Center
    and Dig Sites, 40
Wyoming State Museum,
    38
Wyoming Territorial Prison,
    38
Wyoming Territory, 19, 24

Yellowstone National Park,
    4, 9–10, 14, 20, 35

About the Author

Ann Heinrichs grew up in Fort Smith, Arkansas, and lives in Chicago. She is the author of more than one hundred books for children and young adults on Asian, African, and U.S. history and culture. Ann has also written numerous newspaper, magazine, and encyclopedia articles. She is an award-winning martial artist, specializing in t'ai chi empty-hand and sword forms.

Ann has traveled widely throughout the United States, Africa, Asia, and the Middle East. In exploring each state for this series, she rediscovered the people, history, and resources that make this a great land, as well as the concerns we share with people around the world.